He is Ever Present

By Karen Esteves

KINGSLEY
PUBLISHERS

First published in South Africa by Kingsley Publishers, 2021
Copyright © Karen Esteves, 2021

The right of Karen Esteves to be identified as author of this work has been asserted.

Kingsley Publishers
Pretoria, South Africa
www.kingsleypublishers.com

A catalogue copy of this book will be available from the National Library of South Africa

Paperback ISBN: 978-0-620-91585-4
eBook ISBN: 978-0-620-91586-1

Scripture quotations taken from The Holy Bible, New International Version® NIV®

Copyright © 1973 1978 1984 2011 by Biblica, Inc. TM

Used by permission. All rights reserved worldwide.

All rights reserved. No part of this publication may be reproduced, stored in a retrieval system, or transmitted in any form or by any means – electronic, mechanical, photocopy, recording, or any other – except for brief quotations in printed reviews, without the prior permission of the publisher.

To my family

Table of Contents

Introduction 1

Worthy 2

The Cruel Cross 3

Heaven 5

The Sabbath Day 7

My God The Creator Of All Things 8

Saved By His Blood 10

The Three Angels Message 12

Jesus Is Coming 14

That Day At Calvary 16

In The Garden 18

The Great I Am 20

After Suffering Victory 21

Victory Through Grace 23

Giving God The Glory 25

A New Heart 27

In God's Image 29

Loving Everybody 31

Walking Around Heaven With Jesus 33

He Needs More Than A Coin 35

God Can Use You Too	37
It Was Jesus	39
When We Meet At Our Saviour's Throne	41
The Beauty Of Jesus	43
Name Above All Names	45
Thanks And Praise	47
I Want To Be Like Jesus	48
Higher Than The Mountains	49
Who will you choose?	50
Don't Leave It Too Long	51
Make A Choice	53
God's Love	55
Create In Us A New Heart, Oh God	56
Jesus Lover Of My Soul	58
Jesus In The Storm	59
With Jesus By My Side	61
Joy In The Morning	63
Giving Your Burdens To Jesus	64
What Jesus Can Do	66
Jesus Is Still Near	67
Jesus Walks On The Water	69
In You I Trust	71

In The Hands Of The Potter 72

Kings And Their Kingdoms 74

Starting Life All Over 78

Just One Touch 79

Trim Your Lamps 81

Promises 83

A Little Whispered Prayer 84

The Lost Sheep 85

God's Garden 87

Walking Through The Streets With Jesus 88

When The Lord Comes 90

God's Gifts 92

Now That I Know Jesus 94

Ever Present 96

You Are My God 98

My Light Divine 99

The Heart Of Jesus 100

Hurting 101

A Prayer 103

Acknowledgements 104

About The Author 105

Introduction

One morning while doing my Bible study on Revelation 5 it was suggested that you try express the chapter through a poem or song.

Having always enjoyed poetry I decided to try and write one. Through this I came up with my first poem of the book, entitled WORTHY.

I do believe God helped me and gave me the words to write it and has continued to inspire the words to all the poems since then.

My hope is that my poetry can be a way to give strength and encouragement to people and to share the love of God, to those who need to know that God loves them and a light to those in darkness. Even more so with everything that we have all been through in 2020, there are so many people who are struggling and hurting, and my prayer is that God willing, the words of these poems will touch someone's heart somewhere, in some way.

Worthy

A scroll which no one could open,
no one worthy enough,
Not one who is perfect, spotless and blameless
could open the scroll up above.

But then an angel told me
There is one, who is
perfect, spotless and blameless
and even died on the cross.

Then I looked and saw, a Lamb in front of the throne
with wounds and scars then I knew,
it was He who had suffered and bled and died
to save sinners like me and you.

He died to save each one of us
so we might be saved by His blood,
His name is Jesus and He loves us so much
that He willingly went to the cross.

So blessing, honour, glory, and praise
belong to my Saviour above.

Inspired by Revelation 5

Prayer:

Dear God, I thank you and praise you for your perfect, precious son, Jesus, who was sent to die for us.

The Cruel Cross

He was beaten and bruised,
mocked and scorned,
a crown of thorns
placed on His head,

He carried that cross
upon His back
so weak and in pain
though He was,

His hands and feet were nailed to the cross,
a spear pierced His side,
All this He suffered that day on the cross
was because of His love for us.

He shed His precious blood upon that cross
and died to set us free,
so that we can live eternally,
with Him our Lord and King.

John 19:34

Instead, one of the soldiers pierced Jesus' side with a spear, bringing a sudden flow of blood and water.

Prayer:

Thank you, Lord, that because of your death, we will have eternal life with you.

Heaven

I'll walk around heaven
with Jesus one day
and enjoy all the wonders
He'll have on display.

The streets will be golden,
There'll be diamonds and pearls,
He'll have so much to show me
'twill be quite a thrill.

There'll be lots of animals,
lions and bears,
tigers and monkeys
but we'll have nothing to fear.

There'll be trees with fruit
of every kind to enjoy,
flowers always blooming
oh what a delight.

Then Jesus will show me
the river of life,
that flows from the throne of God
with the tree of life on both sides.

No evil will be there,
no need for the sun,
the Lord God will be the light
shining forth as the Bright Morning Star.

We'll have everything we need and so much more,
we can sit right next to Jesus as He tells of His love,
how He walked amongst men,
healed the sick and the blind.

Oh what stories I can't wait to hear,
so let's do the work that He has for us here.
Let's be prepared for when that great day comes,
so we can all be with Jesus in His mansion above.

Revelation 22:1-21

Then the angel showed me the river of the water of life, as clear as crystal, flowing from the throne of God and of the Lamb down the middle of the great street of the city. On each side of the river stood the tree of life, bearing twelve crops of fruit, yielding its fruit every month. And the leaves of the tree are for the healing of the nations. No longer will there be any curse. The throne of God and of the Lamb will be in the city, and his servants will serve him. They will see his face, and his name will be on their foreheads. There will be no more night. They will not need the light of a lamp or the light of the sun, for the Lord God will give them light. And they will reign for ever and ever....

The Sabbath Day

Holy is the Sabbath day
A day you made for rest,
A day that you have set apart
A day that you have blessed.

You've told us to put aside
our usual daily chores,
to keep this day to spend with you
in worship and in praising.

You want us to observe this day
and remember that it's Holy
and in the end it will be the seal
That shows which path we've chosen.

Mark 2:27-28

Then he said to them, "The Sabbath was made for man, not man for the Sabbath. So the Son of Man is Lord even of the Sabbath

Prayer:

Thank you Lord that you have given us a day to rest at the end of the week, not just to rest but to remind us that you are our creator, the one who made all things.

My God The Creator Of All Things

My God is the creator of all things
from the day to the night,
to the oceans and the heaven
and the sun that shines bright.

He made all the grass and the trees
with fruit bearing seeds,
flowers and birds
and all the fish in the sea.

He made reptiles and cattle,
every kind of wildlife,
like hippo s and jackal
and the yellow billed kite.

Then He made man in His image
from the dust of the earth,
breathed into his nostrils
and gave life without birth.

Last but not least
and the best part of all,
He created the Sabbath
for us all to enjoy.

> He took just seven days
> to create all these things,
> from beginning to end
> He's the King of all Kings.

Genesis 2:1-3

Thus the heavens and the earth were completed in all their vast array.

By the seventh day God had finished the work he had been doing; so on the seventh day he rested from all his work. Then God blessed the seventh day and made it holy, because on it he rested from all the work of creating that he had done.

Prayer:

Thank you Lord for your creation and one day at the end of each week that you have given us to rest on.

Saved By His Blood

The penalty has been paid,
At the cross we were set free,
for our sins He bled and died,
by His blood we've been redeemed.

Through His blood we've been forgiven,
yes, pardoned and released,
the weight of our sins He carries
and by His stripes we are healed.

The price of our salvation
was His death at Calvary,
so I'll put on the great armour
to gain the victory.

First I'll remember the blood of the Lamb
which gives power to overcome,
then I'll use the power of prayer to
get strength from up above.

The strong belt of truth I will share
and the shield will be my faith,
the sword of the Spirit will go with me
and we'll fight 'til victory.

Ephesians 6:13

Therefore put on the full armour of God, so that when the day of evil comes, you may be able to stand your ground, and after you have done everything, to stand.

Prayer:

Lord, please give us strength to stand firm against the attacks of satan.

The Three Angels Message

The message has been sent,
the message that is true,
God has sent His Holy angels
with good news for me and you.

"Fear God" the angel shouted
"and celebrate His greatness",
worship Him who made the heavens and earth
and all of His creations.

Another angel followed,
across the sky he flew,
Shouting, "Babylon has fallen
and the nations are in ruins".

The beast you must not worship,
you must not accept his mark
or you will see God's anger
poured from His cup of wrath.

Help us to remain faithful Lord
and endure patiently,
every trial and terror
'til you come to take us home.

Revelation 14:12

This calls for patient endurance on the part of the people of God who keep his commands and remain faithful to Jesus.

Prayer:

Lord I pray that you will help us stand firm in Your truth.

Jesus Is Coming

No one knows when the Lord will appear
not the day nor the month nor the year.
We know that He'll come like a thief in the night
and we know that His coming is near.

The whole world will see Him surrounded by angels,
We'll hear the trumpets sound,
We'll see Him coming in the clouds
coming to claim His own.

Some will look up filled with joy
some will be filled with fear,
I want to be amongst those filled with joy
and to meet Him in the air.

He'll give us a crown of righteousness
we'll wear a robe of white,
we'll receive the reward He's promised us
and we'll walk on streets of gold.

Oh what love, oh what joy,
oh what peace we'll know,
when we're face to face with Jesus
in our heavenly home.

Matthew 24:42

"Therefore keep watch, because you do not know on what day your Lord will come."

Prayer:

Lord, I pray that each one of us will be ready and waiting eagerly for your soon return.

Help us to live our lives in perfect harmony with you.

That Day At Calvary

That day at the cross
where Jesus suffered and died,
that day at Calvary.

His nail pierced hands,
His nail pierced feet,
To save a wretch like me.

Each drop of blood
was for all my sins,
that day at Calvary

The pain and anguish
that He felt that day
was because of His great love for me.

So I thank you Jesus
for your precious blood that was shed,
that day at Calvary.

1 Peter 2:24

"He himself bore our sins" in his body on the cross, so that we might die to sins and live for righteousness; "by his wounds you have been healed."

Prayer:

I thank you Lord for each drop of blood that was shed for me, that day at Calvary.

In The Garden

In the garden of Gethsemane
Jesus went to pray,
He knew the time was coming
when He would be betrayed.

Peter, James and John
were told to watch and pray,
while Jesus went on further
and to His father prayed.

"May this cup be taken from me
not my will but yours be done"
said Jesus to His father
as He prayed for strength from up above.

He found His disciples sleeping
too tired to watch and pray,
one hour they could not stay awake,
just one hour to watch and pray.

Then Judas arrived with soldiers,
armed with clubs and swords
he betrayed Jesus with a kiss
now prophecy was fulfilled.

Then Jesus was arrested
and led away that day,
to bear our sins upon the cross
for all our sins He'd pay.

But He has risen from the grave,
He's alive, no longer dead.
He will come to take us to live with Him
in the mansion He's prepared.

<u>Matthew 26:42</u>

He went away a second time and prayed, "My Father, if it is not possible for this cup to be taken away unless I drink it, may your will be done."

The Great I Am

Jesus our almighty God sits upon His throne.
He reigns supreme
as our Saviour, Lord and King.
The angels bow before Him
as they worship Him and sing.
We praise you and adore you
for you are The Great I am,
and we lift your name on high.
You are worthy to receive glory, honour and praise,
for you are the name above all names.
You are the one who reigns forever,
you are the Lamb that was slain.

Daniel 2:44

In the time of those kings, the God of heaven will set up a kingdom that will never be destroyed, nor will it be left to another people. It will crush all those kingdoms and bring them to an end, but it will itself endure forever.

Prayer:

Thank you, Lord, that you are our Almighty God, our King, and you reign supreme.

After Suffering Victory

Jesus walked around earth as one of us
He suffered scorn and shame,
He felt temptation and rejection
and though innocent, He was slain.

He took all the blame and suffering,
the humiliation and so much shame.
He took all our sins upon Himself
so that we might all be saved.

On the cross at Calvary
feeling rejected and alone,
by His father He felt forsaken
even though it was not so.

He cried out in a loud voice,
'My God, why have you forsaken me'
and it was then with these words
that He hung His head and died.

But praise God, He rose again,
He's no longer in the grave,
He's alive, He's up in heaven
and He's coming back again.

Luke 24:46

He told them, "This is what is written: The Messiah will suffer and rise from the dead on the third day.

Prayer:

Thank you, Lord, that you have risen from the grave, you have conquered death, and you will come back again to take us to live with you.

Victory Through Grace

My Jesus, my Saviour,
I lift your name on high,
You are the one who came to earth,
You are the one who came to die.

You came to earth as a babe,
You walked and taught on earth,
then you died but rose again
and you are mighty to save.

Mighty Saviour, Wise Counsellor,
Gentle Father you are.
I love you; I adore you
You are my bright and morning star.

You give me joy in the morning,
You give me strength for the day,
You give me hope for tomorrow
and You light up my way.

You give me peace everlasting,
You take away all my fears,
You hold my hand in the darkness
and wipe away all my tears.

Yes, Jesus is my peace and comfort,
He is my joy and my strength,
yes, Jesus is my hope for tomorrow
and my light until the end.

Oh, come my blessed Saviour,
I long to see your face
and then we'll stand in victory
and sing amazing grace.

Philippians 4:13

I can do all this through him who gives me strength.

Prayer:

Thank you, Lord, that we have you, that You love us and You give us the strength we need to overcome obstacles.

Giving God The Glory

I give God the glory,
I worship Him,
for He is my Saviour,
my Lord and my King.

I honour and praise Him
as God's only son,
I give Him glory
and all of my love.

He gives me shelter
from troubles and storms,
He guides me gently
so I won't stumble and fall.

He rains down blessings
from heaven above
and sends down His love,
on the wings of a dove.

He covers me with
His righteous robe
and cleanses me
from all of my sins.

> I am so thankful
> that Jesus came and died for me
> so I will be all
> that He wants me to be.

<u>1John 1:9</u>

If we confess our sins, he is faithful and just and will forgive us our sins and purify us from all unrighteousness.

<u>Prayer:</u>

Thank you, Lord, that you forgive us for our wrongdoings and that you forgive us and cleanse us from all our sins.

A New Heart

Lord I cry out to you
for a heart that is new,
a heart that is pure
and a heart that is true.
I want a heart filled with love
for the lonely and weak,
to lend a kind hand
to the needy and sick.
I want to lighten their burdens,
be a shoulder to cry on.
To lift up the weary
and make their lives brighter.
I want to tell them of Jesus
how He sees every tear,
feels every heartache
and knows all their fears.
I want to tell of your love,
your care and your grace,
forgiveness and mercy,
for the whole human race.

Isaiah 41:10

So do not fear, for I am with you;
do not be dismayed, for I am your God.

I will strengthen you and help you;
I will uphold you with my righteous right hand.

Prayer:

Lord, thank you that you have promised to be with us, to lift us up and carry us through tough times. Please be with those who are going through difficult situations right now.

In God's Image

When God made man in His image
He did not stop to think,
should I make him brown or white
or maybe even pink.

He made him in His likeness
so that man would have His heart,
hearts with love and kindness
was the plan from the very start.

I know He is not concerned
about the colour of our hair,
I know He's not concerned
if it's black or brown or fair.

He simply made us perfect
and His love for us remains,
even though we all look different
inside we're just the same.

Genesis 1:26

Then God said, "Let us make mankind in our image, in our likeness, so that they may rule over the fish in the sea and the birds in the sky, over the livestock and all the wild animals, and over all the creatures that move along the ground."

Prayer:

Thank you for making all things beautiful. Thank you for looking at our hearts rather than the outward appearance.

Loving Everybody

When Jesus said we must love each other,
He was speaking to me and to you,
He said we are to love everybody,
that means our enemies too.

We are to show love through all difficulties,
we are to be kind and merciful too.
Don't let anger get the better of you,
just let God's love shine out of you.

If Jesus can love those who mocked Him
and drove those nails into His hands.
If He can forgive them, for what they did on that day,
then why can't we forgive each other today?

Jesus is the greatest example
of forgiveness, kindness and love
so if you want to be like Jesus
keep your eyes fixed on Him up above.

Luke 6:27

"But to you who are listening I say: Love your enemies, do good to those who hate you,"

Prayer:

Lord help us to show forgiveness towards those who have wronged us, even though it is not always easy.

Walking Around Heaven With Jesus

I can't wait to walk around heaven
with Jesus by my side.
I'll meet Him in the morning
as the sun begins to rise.

We would watch the golden rays
shining brightly in the sky
and listen to the birds sing
in the treetop's way up high.

I would maybe pet a lion
and run my fingers through its mane,
while I hold a little lamb
and pet him just the same.

There would be so many different flowers
with brightly coloured petals,
purple, pink and orange
and some with tiny speckles.

Jesus might pick a daisy
and place it in my hair,
while I sit and listen to Him tell the story
of how He saved us from despair.

Perhaps He would take a walk with me
along the gently flowing river
and we could just talk and talk,
forever and forever.

Oh, I would just love to hear about all the times
He sheltered me from harm,
kept me from pain and sorrow
and held me safely in His palm.

Then as the evening draws nigh
He would give me a warm embrace
and tell me to rest peacefully
peace, in His saving grace.

John 14:2-3

My Father's house has many rooms; if that were not so, would I have told you that I am going there to prepare a place for you? And if I go and prepare a place for you, I will come back and take you to be with me that you also may be where I am.

Prayer:

Thank you, Lord, that we have the hope of being with you in heaven one day. What a time that will be.

He Needs More Than A Coin

I saw him sitting on the sidewalk,
His clothes all tattered and torn.
His feet were bare,
His face was worn
from years of suffering and hardship.
His eyes met mine,
I felt his shame,
as I looked into His weary face.
I saw a glimmer of hope
as he held out his hand,
hands that once laboured before.
Putting my hand in my pocket,
I was about to toss him a coin
but I heard a voice say, 'he needs more than a coin'
so I slowly knelt down by his side.
I placed the coin inside his hand
and held his hand in mine,
then closed my eyes and said a prayer,
to give hope to this child of God.

Psalm 9:18

But God will never forget the needy;
the hope of the afflicted will never perish.

Prayer:

Dear Lord, my prayer today is that you help those that are going through difficult times. Please help them to trust in you to take care of their needs and to know that you love them.

God Can Use You Too

I'm sitting in the garden
watching the bumble bees,
I see them buzzing around and around
in the warm summer breeze.

They land on brightly coloured flowers
and they fly to and fro,
then off they swiftly fly
spreading pollen as they go.

I just love how God uses them
to spread the pollen round,
so that we can have more flowers
growing all around.

God can use us too
just like He uses bees,
to spread His love around
to bring happiness and peace.

Imagine the kind of world
that we would all live in,
if we would spread God's love
how much joy that would bring.

Mark 16:15

He said to them, "Go into all the world and preach the gospel to all creation.

Prayer:

Dear Lord, I pray that you will help us to spread your love around because we know that with your love, we will find peace, joy and contentment.

It Was Jesus

I know a man who walked on the water,
in the midst of the storm, he was there.
When the sea raged around us
we are all so afraid
but then He told us
we had nothing to fear.

This same man who walked on the water
He bade me come unto Him,
I stepped out in faith
but then looked away
and that's when I started to sink.

When I met Jesus out on the water
right there in the midst of the storm,
my heart was afraid
but He held out His hand
and saved me from fear and despair.

It was Jesus, yes, He was there
just as He promised to be.
It was Jesus, yes, He was there,
In the midst of the storm, He was there.

Matthew 14:22-33

Read the entire story

Prayer:

Lord when we are going through difficulties, help us to keep our eyes on you and to have faith that you will be with us.

When We Meet At Our Saviour's Throne

What a day it will be up in heaven
when we meet at our Saviour's throne,
we will sing and rejoice
and lift up our voice
and praise Him in our heavenly home.

We'll sing Holy, Holy, Holy,
Holy is His name.
Worthy, He is worthy,
worthy of honour and praise.

We will bow before our Master
as He sits on His heavenly throne,
We'll sing with love and adoration
and thank Him for taking us home.

We'll sing Holy, Holy, Holy,
Holy is His name.
Worthy, He is worthy
worthy of honour and praise.

We will sit at the feet of our Saviour
as He sits on His heavenly throne,
we'll sing with the angels in chorus
and celebrate that we're finally home.

We'll sing Holy, Holy, Holy,
Lord God almighty.
Worthy, He is worthy
worthy of honour and praise.

Isaiah 43:15

"I am the Lord, your Holy One,
Israel's Creator, your King."

The Beauty Of Jesus

How beautiful are the feet of Jesus,
how marvellous are His ways.
He walked in the footsteps of His father
when on earth He came to stay.

Birthed by the blessed virgin Mary,
sent by His father God on high,
down to earth He came to perish,
for all our sins He came to die.

How beautiful are the hands of Jesus,
those hands were nailed to the cross,
the hands that touched the blind and healed them
when He came to seek and save the lost.

He came to bear our sins and sorrows,
yes, He died but conquered death,
now He's alive, He's up in heaven
but He's coming back again.

How beautiful is the heart of Jesus,
a heart that's filled with agape love.
A love that's patient, pure and tender
and it overflows from His throne above.

1 Corinthians 15:20

But Christ has indeed been raised from the dead, the firstfruits of those who have fallen asleep.

Prayer:

Thank you, Lord, that you love us so much that you came to this earth as our example and then died for our sins.

Name Above All Names

The Lord is our creator,
the Prince of peace is He.
He's our Saviour, our Messiah,
He's everything to me.

He's the King of Kings and Lord of Lords,
The Living Word is He.
He is the Son of God,
second person in the Trinity

He's our Saviour, our Redeemer,
He's our comforter and friend.
He's the Alpha and Omega,
the Beginning and the End.

Isaiah 9:6

For to us a child is born,
to us a son is given,
and the government will be on his shoulders.
And he will be called
Wonderful Counselor, Mighty God,
Everlasting Father, Prince of Peace.

Meditation:

Make Jesus Christ your Lord, Saviour, Mighty God, and friend and first in everything you do, then you will find peace and comfort and all you will ever need.

Thanks And Praise

Thank you, Father, for all that you give,
for clothes on my back and shoes on my feet,
for safety and warmth through the cold dark night,
and a heart that is healthy and filled with your love.
A roof over my head and food to eat,
family to love, to cherish and keep.
So, I'll thank you Father again and again
for all that you do and all that you give.

Psalm 100 :4-5

Enter his gates with thanksgiving
and his courts with praise;
give thanks to him and praise his name.
For the Lord is good and his love endures forever;
his faithfulness continues through all generations.

Meditation:

Think about all the things you have been blessed with. Good health, strength, employment, family and the many more things we have been blessed with and give thanks to God for all you have.

The Lord loves a grateful heart.

I Want To Be Like Jesus

I want to love you Lord
the way you want me to.
I want to follow your example
to be loving, kind, and true.
I want to let my light shine
in all I say and do.
I want to be the kind of person
that you want me to be,
so I can one day live with you
for all eternity.

1John 2:6

Whoever claims to live in him must live as Jesus did.

Prayer:

Lord help me to put aside all that is keeping me from becoming more like you. Thank you for being our example.

Higher Than The Mountains

Higher than the mountains,
deeper than the sea,
wider than the ocean
is God's great love for me.
It's everlasting and so strong,
it's kind and gentle too.
It's amazing, its omnipotent,
merciful and true.

John 3:16

For God so loved the world that he gave his one and only Son, that whoever believes in him shall not perish but have eternal life.

Meditation:

Always remember that God's love for you is so great, that He gave up His only Son to die for you. There is nothing you can ever do to make Him stop loving you.

Who will you choose?

Jesus is giving you time to decide,
who will you choose,
will you be on His side?

He has shown us His way
through God's Holy Word,
so you can decide who to serve.

Jesus is waiting for you to choose,
the way of the world
or the way of His truth.

He has shown us His way
through His loving care
so you can decide who you'll serve.

He has shown us His love by His death on the cross,
so who will you choose,
who will you serve?

John 14:6

Jesus answered, "I am the way and the truth and the life. No one comes to the Father except through me.

Prayer:

Lord, please help me to follow your way. Help me to choose you as my Lord and Saviour.

Don't Leave It Too Long

Open your heart
and invite Jesus in,
He's patiently waiting
for you to let Him come in.

Time is too short,
it's passing you by,
open your ears
and you will hear His faint cry.

He's pleading with you
to come back to Him,
He's waiting for you
to turn from your sin.

Don't leave it too long,
don't waste any time,
He wants you to be part
of His heavenly throng.

Matthew 18:12

"What do you think? If a man owns a hundred sheep, and one of them wanders away, will he not leave the ninety-nine on the hills and go to look for the one that wandered off?"

Prayer:

Lord, I want you to be part of my life. Please help me to accept you into my life. I choose you today. Thank you for loving me.

Make A Choice

Who will you put your faith in,
let's make our choice today.
Will it be our Lord and Saviour,
who can give us hope today?

Just talk to Him and ask Him
to come into your life
and He will step right in
with His arms stretched open wide.

He's knocking at your door
He wants to be let in,
He's waiting for you to open up
so He can step right in.

He wants you to make that choice,
He wants to set you free,
He wants to take you home
where you'll live eternally.

He wants you to be ready,
He wants you to be on time.
Don't hesitate, don't wait too long
Because time flies quickly by.

Revelation 3:20

Here I am! I stand at the door and knock. If anyone hears my voice and opens the door, I will come in and eat with that person, and they with me.

Prayer:

Lord, please come into my heart; I want to accept you into my life. Thank you for never giving up on me.

God's Love

Lord you gave us knees to bow before you
and hands to fold in prayer,
You gave us eyes to close tightly
as we bow our heads in prayer.

You gave us lips to sing Your praises
and to talk to You each day,
You gave us ears to hear your voice
as you guide us along our way.

You gave us a heart to love and a mind to think
of those who need our care,
so that we might do as you did
and help save them from despair.

Ephesians 2:10

For we are God's handiwork, created in Christ Jesus to do good works, which God prepared in advance for us to do.

Prayer:

Please help me Lord to do your will. Thank you for the gifts you have given me to use that I may do your work.

Create In Us A New Heart, Oh God

Will we make some changes
in this sinful world today?
Will we heed the warning of the Lord
and hasten to obey?

Or will it be like in Noah's day
when men were wicked and depraved,
carrying hate within their hearts
and not willing to obey.

Will we repent before it's too late,
from all our worldly ways?
Will we ask Jesus to cleanse us
and renew us day by day?

Create in us a new heart oh God,
cleanse us from within,
make us more like Jesus
because we want to be like Him.

Psalm 51:10

Create in me a pure heart, O God,
and renew a steadfast spirit within me.

Prayer:

Lord, I ask that you change my heart today. Please help me to be obedient

And make me more like you.

Jesus Lover Of My Soul

Jesus lover of my soul,
help my eyes to see
the little things that I can do
to be your hands and feet.

Help my heart to feel Lord
for some weary troubled soul,
help me to lift them up Lord
and guide them to your fold.

Let me be a shining light
for everyone to see,
so that Jesus can be seen
shining out from me.

Jesus lover of my soul
fall afresh on me.

Matthew 5:16

In the same way, let your light shine before others, that they may see your good deeds and glorify your Father in heaven.

Prayer:

Lord, I ask that you help me to be a shining light, not for my glory but so that others can see you in me.

Jesus In The Storm

Evening was coming,
the sun was sinking low,
so they climbed into the boat
and they began to row.

Jesus was feeling tired
and decided to take a nap,
so He lay down in the boat
as they rowed across the lake.

But very soon a storm arose
and water filled the boat
but Jesus lay there sound asleep,
as they struggled to keep afloat.

The disciples in their frightened state
woke Jesus from His sleep,
shouting, "Teacher, do you not care,
that we're about to sink?"

Then Jesus stood up and raised His hand,
"Peace be still", He said, and suddenly it was calm.
The winds stopped thrashing; the waves stopped crashing.
They were obeying His command.

Then Jesus turned to them and asked,
"Why were you afraid, don't you have faith in me yet"?
The disciples looked at Him in awe and wondered,
who was this man, that even the winds and waves obey Him?

Mark 4:39

He got up, rebuked the wind and said to the waves, "Quiet! Be still!" Then the wind died down and it was completely calm.

Prayer:

Please help us to trust you, Lord.

With Jesus By My Side

I never have to feel afraid
with Jesus by my side.
I never have to feel alone
because His arms are open wide.

I only have to talk to Him
and tell Him all my fears.
I only have to run to Him
to feel His warm embrace.

He longs for us to take to Him
our worries and our cares.
He wants to give us comfort
and wipe away our tears.

So, if you're going through some struggles
and don't know what to do,
give them all to Jesus,
because He will see you through.

Joshua 1:9

"Have I not commanded you? Be strong and courageous. Do not be afraid; do not be discouraged, for the Lord your God will be with you wherever you go."

Prayer:

Thank you, Lord that we can give all our worries and burdens to you.

Joy In The Morning

You give me joy in the morning,
You give me strength for the day,
You give me hope for tomorrow,
and light that lights up my way.

You give me peace everlasting,
You take away all of my fear,
You hold my hand in the darkness,
and You wipe away all my tears.

Yes, Jesus is my peace and comfort,
He is my joy and my strength,
Yes, Jesus is my hope for tomorrow,
and my light until the end.

Romans 15:13

May the God of hope fill you with all joy and peace as you trust in him, so that you may overflow with hope by the power of the Holy Spirit.

Prayer:

Lord, thank you that we can find peace and joy in you.

Giving Your Burdens To Jesus

Sometimes we take the longest road
with all its twists and turns,
then stop to load some baggage on,
at each and every curve.

We pick it up and pack it in,
with a little unforgiveness,
then around the bend we stop again,
to load on hurt and bitterness.

When it's nicely packed,
we lift it up; and carry it around,
not stopping once to offload
the burdens that abound.

With each and every step we take
the load just weighs us down,
until we cannot bear the strain
and we fall down to the ground.

This is just the place we should be,
right there upon our knees,
giving Jesus all our burdens,
and telling Him all our needs.

> He will help us offload bitterness,
> unforgiveness, hurt and pain.
> Give us joy, peace and comfort,
> to get us through each day.

Psalm 55:22

Cast your cares on the Lord
and he will sustain you;
he will never let
the righteous be shaken.

Prayer:

Thank you, God, that you are willing to carry each one of our burdens for us. Help us to give them all to you.

What Jesus Can Do

Jesus will calm your worries and fears,
as He calmed the raging sea.
He lifted His hands and said, "Peace be still"
on the sea of Galilee.

Jesus will give you comfort,
and fill your heart with gladness.
He will wrap His arms around you,
and take away your sadness.

Jesus can take a heart of stone,
and make it soft and tender,
and fill it with His love;
so, it to others you can render.

Ezekiel 36:26

I will give you a new heart and put a new spirit in you; I will remove from you your heart of stone and give you a heart of flesh.

Prayer:

Thank you, Lord, that you calm our worries, you comfort us when we are sad and you can give us a heart of flesh, filled with love for others.

Jesus Is Still Near

In the middle of the worlds struggles,
people run to and fro,
searching for something;
but, don't know which way to go.

There's suffering, turmoil
and financial crises.
Evil deeds , pestilences,
earthquakes and fires.

People no longer
have love in their heart;
but, anger, hate,
rebellion and strife.

People refuse to listen
and turn from their sins;
but we can still trust and believe,
in God's Holy Word.

In the midst of our struggles,
Jesus is near.
He hears and He answers,
each one of our prayers.

Luke 21:11

There will be great earthquakes, famines and pestilences in various places, and fearful events and great signs from heaven.

Prayer:

Dear Lord help us not to be fearful but to remember that in our struggles you are always near

Jesus Walks On The Water

Jesus walked on the water
out on the lake;
in the midst of a storm,
just before daybreak.

Peter and his friends
trying to keep afloat,
became really afraid,
when a storm rocked their boat.

Then they saw Jesus,
and cried out in terror;
but Jesus told them,
they had nothing to fear.

Lord, if it really is you,
let me walk on the water.
Then Jesus said, "Come,
but don't let your feet falter."

So, Peter stepped out of the boat,
and walked towards Jesus;
but then began to sink,
and fear was the reason.

"Save me Lord", Peter shouted.
Jesus reached out His hand
and saved him from drowning.
"Oh man of little faith," Jesus said,
"Why did you doubt me?"

Matthew 14:27

But Jesus immediately said to them, "Take courage! It is I, do not be afraid."

In You I Trust

We know, Lord Jesus, you always provide,
for all our daily needs, you do supply.
You fill all of our daily needs,
and answer each one of our urgent pleas.
You touch our hearts
with your healing words,
through your precious promises, I am assured.
We know in you, we can have faith,
so, I'll trust in your amazing grace.

Hebrews 11:1

Now faith is confidence in what we hope for and assurance about what we do not see.

In The Hands Of The Potter

Jesus is the Potter; we are the clay.
If you ask Him to,
He will mould you and shape you,
in His own way.

He'll smooth you out, shape you
into someone quite new,
filling the chips;
and the cracks He will smooth.

Your heart He will touch
and fill with His love.
Then mould you and make you,
out of His heart of love.

He will smooth out the bitterness, anger and untruths,
then fill in the cracks caused by jealousy too.
He will replace the hurt, with His grace and His love;
and fill you with His goodness sent from above.

He does not need clay,
He does not need glue,
because He will just give you
a heart that is new.

Isaiah 64:8

Yet you, Lord, are our Father.
We are the clay, you are the potter;
we are all the work of your hand.

Prayer:

Lord, I pray that you make me into what you want me to be.

Kings And Their Kingdoms

Right down through the ages
we've seen kingdoms rise; and we've seen kingdoms fall.
Kings come and go,
Kings been destroyed,

Idolatry and murder,
were the norm amongst Kings.
Slavery, cruelty,
and all those wicked things.

King Solomon with all his wisdom,
turned away from God.
He began worshipping idols,
then saw God's anger unfold.

Then there was King Ahab,
the King of Israel.
Who went against God's wishes
and married Jezebel.

To make matters worse,
he followed HER way.
He began worshipping idols,
after she led him astray.

Kings and their kingdoms,
adultery and strife.
Remember King David,
who stole Uriah's wife?

Then there was King Herod,
the most wicked of all.
He reigned in Judea,
at the time Jesus was born.

Herod became worried
when he heard the news,
that a baby was born,
who would be King of the Jews?

Then Herod plotted to kill all boys under two,
but God knew Herod's plan.
He sent Mary and Joseph,
to a far distant land

Kings and their kingdoms,
their riches of gold.
Ivory and silver,
and all of their wealth.

But our King Jesus,
humble and meek,
was born in a stable,
surrounded by cattle and sheep.

Unlike the Kings
in those days of old,
He had no riches, no wealth,
no silver or gold

In that manger lay the baby,
who would one day be our King.
We would bow and worship Him,
as our Saviour, Lord and King.

The Kings of this earth,
rule with fear and with force,
but Jesus our King,
gives freedom of choice.

Our King Jesus is our peace, our comfort,
our joy and strength.
He's our hope for tomorrow,
our light until the end.

Right down through the ages,
we've seen kingdoms rise and we've seen kingdoms fall.
Kings come and go.
Kings being destroyed.

Our King Jesus has set up a kingdom,
that will never be destroyed.
A kingdom that will last forever,
a kingdom where we'll live forevermore.

Exodus 15:18

"The Lord reigns
for ever and ever."

Starting Life All Over

So many years of suffering
and pain within my heart.
Help me Lord to start over,
to make a brand-new start.

Though my days are rough, my nights are long
and my journey has been a struggle.
Lord, please give me strength to overcome,
so, I'll have victory over sorrow.

"My child I see your heartache
and each burden that you carry.
Just trust in me, and I'll show you
how to start your life all over.

Just give me all your troubles,
don't worry over them,
be like the little sparrows,
they don't worry about a thing."

Luke 12:7

Indeed, the very hairs of your head are all numbered. Don't be afraid; you are worth more than many sparrows.

Prayer:

Thank you, Lord that you care so very much for each one of us.

Just One Touch

She had been sick for far too long,
twelve years of suffering and shame.
Just getting worse as time went by
trying to hide her shame.

Joining the crowd that followed Jesus,
having faith that He'd make her well.
Just one touch is all I need.
Just one touch of His robe.

As she got close, she reached out her hand;
touching the hem of His garment.
Just by that touch, she knew right away,
that a miracle had just happened that day.

Immediately Jesus turned and looked at the crowd.
"Who touched my garment?" He asked.
Then the frightened woman came and fell at His feet,
"Master, it was I" she replied.
Jesus gently said,
"Daughter, go in peace, your faith has made you well."

Mark 5:28-29

because she thought, "If I just touch his clothes, I will be healed." Immediately her bleeding stopped and she felt in her body that she was freed from her suffering.

Prayer:

Lord I ask that you help us to touch the hem of your garment through our prayers and our faith in you. Let us not separate ourselves from you, but to reach out and take hold of you in our struggles, trusting you to help us in all things.

Trim Your Lamps

Trim your lamps and keep them burning,
the Bridegroom will soon be here.
Do not slumber or grow weary,
the wedding will soon take place.

We see the turmoil and trouble around us,
signs that His coming is near.
But if you keep your faith in Him,
then you have nothing to fear.

Do not let your lamps grow dim,
Do not feel discouraged,
just trim your lamps and keep them burning,
the Bridegroom will soon appear.

One day we'll look up heavenward.
Oh, what glory we'll behold,
so keep your eyes fixed on Him,
He's coming to take us home.

Matthew 25:6

"At midnight the cry rang out: 'Here's the bridegroom! Come out to meet him!'

Prayer:

Dear Lord, help us to keep awake, to keep our lamps burning and to be ready for your soon return.

Promises

Lord, you have given us many promises.
A promise of protection,
A promise of peace,
A promise of joy
and many blessings to keep.
You have promised to be our refuge,
our strength when we are weak,
a help in times of trouble,
Our comforter and friend.

John 16:33

"I have told you these things, so that in me you may have peace. In this world you will have trouble. But take heart! I have overcome the world."

Prayer:

Thank you, Lord, for your precious promises.

A Little Whispered Prayer

Do you feel discouraged,
loaded down with worries and cares?
Take it to the Lord,
in a little whispered prayer.

He will hear your cry,
He is your comfort and your strength,
so take it to the Lord
in a little whispered prayer.

Are you tired and weak;
and feel you can't go on?
Take it to the lord,
for He's a friend indeed.

1Peter 5:7

Cast all your anxiety on him because he cares for you.

Prayer:

Thank you, Lord, that we can come to you with all our worries and cares.

The Lost Sheep

Ninety-nine sheep gathered.
Ninety-nine sheep locked away for the night.
All but one is put away safely.
All but one is safe and sound.

The shepherd searched all night long,
till that one lost sheep was found.
Over hills and in valleys,
behind bushes, under rocks and in crannies.

The same thing happens in Heaven,
not one sheep who has wandered,
will be left alone and uncared for,
not one does the Good Shepherd ignore.

There's great joy in heaven over that one lost sheep,
who has come back into the fold.
Such joy over that one sheep, who had gone astray
but returned to the Shepherd at last.

Saviour, like a shepherd keep us
ever so near to your heart.
Help me to walk in your footsteps,
may our love for you never depart.

Luke 15:7

I tell you that in the same way there will be more rejoicing in heaven over one sinner who repents than over ninety-nine righteous persons who do not need to repent.

Prayer:

Thank you, Lord, that you never give up on us. Please help us to hear your still, small voice beckoning us to come back to you.

God's Garden

I'll tend God's garden here on earth,
by scattering seeds all around.
Seeds of love and seeds of hope
sent from up above.

I'll water them and watch them sprout,
I'll nurture them with care.
I'll do the work He's asked me to,
then prayerfully watch and wait.

God sees the work we do for Him,
He sees each planted seed.
He has a plan for each new bud,
as they grow in love for Him.

Prayer:

Help us Lord to do your work and spread your word around. My prayer is that every person will have an opportunity to know Jesus as their Saviour and friend.

Walking Through The Streets With Jesus

If we could have walked with Jesus
along the streets of Galilee.
We would have seen some miracles
He performed along the way.

We would have seen Him heal the lame
and make the blind to see.
We would have seen Him heal the sick,
as He touched them tenderly.

If we could have walked with Jesus
along those dusty roads,
we would have seen Him comfort those
who were carrying heavy loads.

We could have followed Him up the hillside,
and sat and listened as He preached;
and taught us how to live
to find happiness and peace

He would have told us how we should live for Him,
to be humble, kind, and meek.
To be loving and forgiving,
and to show mercy to the weak.

> We could have taken a rest with Him
> under a big old shady tree,
> and listened as He told us
> of His great love for you and me.

Jeremiah 30:17

But I will restore you to health
and heal your wounds,'
declares the Lord,
'because you are called an outcast,
Zion for whom no one cares.'

Prayer:

Lord, we know that sometimes to heal, we have to go through some very difficult parts of our lives but we know through you, there is always light at the end of the tunnel.

When The Lord Comes

No one knows when the Lord will appear,
not the day or the month or the year.
We know that He'll come like a thief in the night,
and we know that His coming is near.

The whole world will see Him, surrounded by angels,
we'll hear the trumpets sound.
We'll see Him coming in the clouds,
coming to claim His own.

Some will look up filled with joy,
some will be filled with fear.
I want to be amongst those filled with joy,
and to meet Him in the air.

He'll give us a crown of righteousness,
we'll wear a robe of white.
We'll receive the reward He's promised us,
and we'll walk on streets of gold.

Oh, what love, Oh, what joy,
Oh, what peace we'll know.
When we're face to face with Jesus,
in our heavenly home.

Mark 13:33

Be on guard! Be alert! You do not know when that time will come.

Prayer:

Please help us to live our lives in such a way that it will be pleasing to you. Help us to be ready and waiting to receive the gift of eternal life with you.

God's Gifts

Lord, I watch the ripples of the water,
I see the sky so blue,
the trees so green, the blossoming flowers,
and I know they're made by you.

Your hands have made the beauty
that we see all around.
The birds that fly, the fish that swim,
the tigers and elephants too.

There's so much more to marvel at,
like the stars that light up the sky.
The big bright sun that warms the day,
and the moon that shines at night.

The rain that falls from the clouds up high,
to water the earth below,
but these are just some of the things,
sent from our Father above.

There are just so many gifts to be thankful for,
but the greatest gift,
the most perfect gift,
is the gift of God's only son.

John 1:3

Through him all things were made; without him nothing was made that has been made.

Prayer:

Thank you, Lord, The Creator of all things, for all beauty all around us. Thank you for the perfect gift of Jesus.

Now That I Know Jesus

Coming from a life of poverty and hardship,
no tender comforting touch.
Only feelings of hunger
and often the lash of a belt.

Then one day a lady came,
and gave me food to eat.
She told me about Jesus love,
and how He died for me.

She took me into her home,
and gave me a place to sleep;
and now I have felt that tender touch,
and I know that she loves me.

She told me that Jesus loves me,
and that I'll never be alone,
because I have a friend in Jesus,
and He's my very own.

And now that I know Jesus,
I have a friend in Him,
because in my time of need, He sent my guardian angel,
to come and rescue me.

Matthew 25:35

For I was hungry and you gave me something to eat, I was thirsty and you gave me something to drink, I was a stranger and you invited me in.

Prayer:

Please help us to remember Lord, that when we do for others, we are doing for you

This poem is dedicated to a friend of mine, who fostered a little boy who came from a life of real poverty and hardship.

Ever Present

When you walk next to Jesus,
He'll show you the way.
When you hold on to His hand,
He won't let you stray.

He will guide you gently
through struggles and storms,
holding you up
so that you will not fall.

He'll give you courage and comfort
to pass through the fire,
walking with you
through the mud and the mire.

He is forever present,
ever so near.
Just trust in Him,
and you'll have nothing to fear.

Psalm 46:1

God is our refuge and strength,
an ever-present help in trouble.

Prayer:

Thank you, Lord, that we only have to call out your name and you hear us and will help us.

You Are My God

You are my God in whom I trust,
my strength and comfort,
the one on whom I can depend.

You are my Light,
my light divine,
the light that lights up my way.

My joy, my hope,
the Prince of peace,
my Saviour and my friend.

The living water,
the bread of life
where I go to find sweet rest.

John 6:35

Then Jesus declared, "I am the bread of life. Whoever comes to me will never go hungry, and whoever believes in me will never be thirsty."

Prayer:

Help us Lord, to feed on the bread of life and drink from the living water, who is our Lord, Jesus, Christ. Then we will find our joy, peace, and strength.

My Light Divine

Lord, guide me along the rocky trails,
please take my hand and lead the way.
Help my feet to never falter,
as I wade through the muddy water.
May I keep my eyes fixed on you,
and may my heart stay forever true.
As we walk along together,
we will face the stormy weather.
I know, with your hand in mine,
you will be my Light Divine.

Luke 1:37

For no word from God will ever fail.

Prayer:

Lord, please be with those who are going through difficult times. Help them to take hold of your hand and to know that you will never let them go.

The Heart Of Jesus

The gentle heart of Jesus can heal a wounded soul.
The caring heart of Jesus will comfort those who mourn.
The watchful eyes of Jesus see all our hurts and pains,
and the loving heart of Jesus, will take all those hurts away.
He knows we do not have the strength, to carry them about,
but if we go to Him and ask Him,
He will lift us up, and carry us,
to make those burdens light.

Isaiah 46:4

Even to your old age and gray hairs
I am he, I am he who will sustain you.
I have made you and I will carry you;
I will sustain you and I will rescue you.

Prayer:

Thank you, Lord

Hurting

Troubles always seem to come my way
from when I was a child.
I could not fully understand
what I felt inside

There's an emptiness that I feel,
it hurts from deep within.
My heart is aching from that void,
I just long to feel complete.

I try so hard to avoid the hurt,
keeping it inside,
pushing it down deep,
Where it festers from within.

I want my heart to heal,
I want to feel at peace,
I want to overcome the hurt,
and feel the sweet release.

Help me Lord, please give me strength,
wrap your arms around me.
Lead me to a safe place,
where I'll feel your love surround me.

Psalm 34:18

The Lord is close to the brokenhearted
and saves those who are crushed in spirit.

Prayer:

Lord Jesus, I pray for those going through troubles, hurts and suffering. I think of the those that don't have family, the elderly, the lonely. Lord we are so grateful for your abounding love for each one of us. So, I pray that they will feel your presence with them always.

A Prayer

I pray we find peace in the chaos,
Love in our struggles,
Hope in the darkness,
Healing in our hearts,
and Jesus in the storm.

Acknowledgements

First, I would like to thank my Lord Jesus for giving me the words to express His love for us all through poetry. My loving husband Jose, for his patience and encouragement through the many late nights. To my three children and their spouses for taking the time to read my poems and for all their encouraging words. A big thank you to my grandson for his technical support.

A special thanks to Kingsley Publishing for your professional guidance and creative input.

Thank you for believing in my dream.

To my family and friends who have supported me, I appreciate you all.

About The Author

Karen Esteves is a South African born Author originating from KwaZulu Natal. For the past three years Karen and her family have been living in New Zealand.

She is blessed with a wonderful husband, three children and three beautiful grandchildren with her fourth grandchild on his way.

Karen's heart has always been drawn to teaching children, looking after the elderly and helping those in need.

Karen prays the words in her poetry will touch hearts and encourage those in need of upliftment.

LIKE Karen's page on Facebook : @KarenEstevesAuthor and let her know what you think of her book. She would love to hear from you!

www.ingramcontent.com/pod-product-compliance
Lightning Source LLC
Chambersburg PA
CBHW022120040426
42450CB00006B/783